JAZZ TOGETHER
for one piano, four hands

by Arletta O'Hearn

KJOS Neil A. Kjos Music Company • San Diego, California

About the composer

    Arletta O'Hearn is an independent piano teacher in Portland, Oregon, teaching both jazz and classical repertoire. She performs three nights a week as the pianist in a professional jazz quartet. She is an active member of the Portland chapter of the Oregon Music Teachers Association, through which she is state certified.

    Mrs. O'Hearn has received the Award of Merit from the National Federation of Music Clubs for American Music and was chosen 1984 "Composer of the Year" by the Oregon Music Teachers Association.

Piano Music by Arletta O'Hearn

Jazz Theme and Variations (two pianos)
Jazz Together (one piano, four hands)
Love Jazz
Sunshine and Blues

Lullaby 4

The tempo of this piece should be slow and loving. I have indicated some measures needing a slight stress on beat 4 in the Primo, but always gentle. The piece follows the ABA form. At measure 21 there is a little conversation between Primo and Secondo that should be emphasized. The pedal changes should occur with each change in harmony, ending with a longer held pedal for measures 31 and 32.

Waltz 6

This piece needs the feeling of "swing," but never faster than the metronome marking of 92. There is a great deal of conversation between Primo and Secondo throughout, which should be brought out. The pedaling should follow the harmonic changes, ending with a longer pedal for the last two measures. Perhaps the students can have fun finding the many major and minor 7ths and 9ths!

Scherzo 10

This piece is the most challenging of the set. The eighth notes are not relaxed, but exactly as written. It is bright and fast and more percussive in sound, so the pedal should be used sparingly. Rests are to be strictly observed. At measure 17 the feeling is more lyrical, so pedals can be longer until measure 32. There should be no ritardando at the end, just the fermata.

Nothin' But the Blues 14

Again I have written the relaxed swing style, this time in blues. The relaxed eighth notes written ♪♪ can also be interpreted ♪♪. The important thing is that they remain legato. At measure 14, the same applies to both hands in Primo and Secondo, always legato. Outside of mp for the first 12 bars and mf for the second 12 bars, I have not indicated any shading in dynamics, but the students are welcome to add any they prefer.

ISBN 0-8497-5230-2

© 1983 Kjos West, 4382 Jutland Drive, San Diego, California. International copyright secured.
Printed in U.S.A.

Lullaby

Arletta O'Hearn

© 1983 Kjos West

Waltz

Arletta O'Hearn

Scherzo

Arletta O'Hearn

Nothin' But the Blues

Arletta O'Hearn